Reinforcement Learning for Coders

Enhancing Programming Efficiency with AI-Driven Techniques

Benjamin Evans

DEDICATION

To the relentless seekers of knowledge, the curious minds tirelessly decoding the mysteries of algorithms and code. This book is dedicated to you, the coders who embrace the challenges of Reinforcement Learning with fervor and determination. May these pages serve as stepping stones on your journey, empowering you to unravel the complexities of this dynamic field and craft solutions that shape the future. Your passion fuels the innovation that drives our world forward, and for that, I extend my deepest gratitude and admiration.

CONTENTS

ACKNOWLEDGMENTS

I would like to extend my sincere gratitude to all those who have contributed to the realization of this book. First and foremost, I am indebted to my family for their unwavering support and encouragement throughout this endeavor. Their love and understanding have been my anchor in the stormy seas of writing.

I am deeply thankful to the experts whose guidance and insights have illuminated my path and enriched the content of this book. Their mentorship has been invaluable in shaping my understanding and refining my ideas.

I also extend my appreciation to those whose constructive feedback and insightful suggestions have helped polish this work to its finest form.

Furthermore, I am grateful to the countless individuals whose research, publications, and contributions have paved the way for the insights shared in these pages.

Last but not least, I express my heartfelt appreciation to the readers who embark on this journey with me. Your curiosity and engagement breathe life into these words, and it is for you that this book exists.

Thank you all for being part of this remarkable journey.

CHAPTER 1

Introduction to Reinforcement Learning (RL)

Welcome to the exciting world of reinforcement learning (RL) and its potential to revolutionize how you code! In this chapter, we'll delve into the fundamentals of RL, explore its core concepts, and understand how it can significantly enhance your programming efficiency.

1.1 What is Reinforcement Learning?

Unlike traditional programming approaches where you explicitly instruct the computer what to do, RL takes a different path. Imagine training an animal through rewards and punishments. Similarly, RL agents (computer programs) learn by interacting with an environment and receiving feedback. This feedback comes in the form of rewards for desirable actions and penalties for undesirable ones. Over time, through trial and error, the agent learns to navigate the environment and maximize its reward.

Here's a breakdown of the key players in RL:

Agent: This is the learning program you create. It interacts with the environment and takes actions.

Environment: This is the world or situation the agent operates in. It provides feedback to the agent in the form of rewards and penalties.

Actions: These are the choices the agent can make within the environment.

Rewards: These are positive reinforcements that encourage the agent to repeat specific actions.

Penalties: These are negative consequences that discourage the agent from taking certain actions.

Through this continuous cycle of action, feedback, and learning, RL agents can develop remarkable abilities to solve complex problems without explicit instructions.

1.2 Core Concepts in RL: Agents, Environments, Rewards, and Actions

Let's delve deeper into the core concepts that make RL tick:

Agents: You, as the programmer, design the agent. You define its capabilities for perception, action, and learning. For coding tasks, the agent could analyze code structure, generate code snippets, or suggest optimizations.

Environments: The environment in coding could be your development platform, a specific codebase, or even a simulated coding challenge. The environment provides the agent with information about the current state (e.g., current line of code) and allows it to take actions (e.g., suggest a code completion).

Rewards: Rewards are crucial for guiding the agent's learning. In coding, a reward might be given for generating a bug-free code snippet or optimizing code performance.

Actions: Actions are the choices the agent makes within the environment. These could be completing a code line, suggesting a library import, or refactoring existing code for better efficiency.

By carefully defining these core elements, you can shape the agent's learning process and equip it to tackle specific coding challenges.

1.3 Benefits of RL for Programmers

Here's how RL can transform your coding experience:

Automation of Repetitive Tasks: RL agents can automate repetitive coding tasks like generating test cases, fixing common bugs, or suggesting code refactoring techniques. This frees you to focus on more creative and strategic aspects of programming.

Improved Code Quality: RL agents can be trained to identify and suggest improvements to your code, leading to cleaner, more efficient, and maintainable codebases.

Personalized Coding Assistance: Imagine an AI assistant that understands your coding style and project goals. RL agents can be personalized to provide context-aware suggestions and complete tasks based on your specific needs.

Faster Learning and Experimentation: RL allows you to experiment with different coding approaches without manually re-writing code. This accelerates your learning process and helps you discover optimal solutions faster.

1.4 Real-World Applications of RL in Coding

The possibilities are vast! Here are some real-world applications of RL in coding:

1. Automating code generation for simple tasks.
2. Learning to write unit tests that effectively cover different code functionalities.
3. Suggesting code optimizations based on performance benchmarks.
4. Identifying and fixing bugs in code by learning patterns in successful code fixes.

As RL technology continues to evolve, we can expect even more innovative applications that transform how we code and create software.

CHAPTER 2

DEMYSTIFYING RL ALGORITHMS

Now, it's time to unveil the magic behind the scenes - the algorithms that power these learning agents. This chapter dives into some popular RL algorithms commonly used for coding tasks, making them understandable for programmers without a deep background in machine learning.

2.1 Q-Learning: Learning Through Trial and Error

Imagine a programmer learning a new coding language. They experiment with different approaches, observing the outcomes (positive or negative) and gradually refining their strategy. Q-Learning operates with a similar principle.

Here's how it works:

Q-table: The agent maintains a Q-table, essentially a large lookup table. Each entry in the table represents a state (e.g., current line of code) and an action (e.g., suggest a code completion). The value stored in the table (Q-value) signifies the expected reward for taking that action in that specific state.

Exploration vs. Exploitation: During training, the agent explores the environment by trying different actions in various states. It updates the Q-values based on the rewards received. Initially, exploration dominates as the agent learns the environment. Over time, it exploits its knowledge by favoring actions with higher Q-values (actions that have historically led to better rewards).

Example: Imagine a simple coding environment where the agent learns to identify the correct data type for a variable. The state could be "declaring a new variable," and the actions could be "int," "float," or "string." The reward could be +1 for choosing the correct data type and -1 for choosing the wrong one. The Q-table would gradually update based on the rewards, guiding the agent towards suggesting the best data type in different scenarios.

Code Snippet (Simplified):

python

```
# Initialize Q-table with zeros
    Q = np.zeros((num_states, num_actions))


    for episode in range(num_episodes):
      state = starting_state
      while not is_terminal(state):


# Choose action based on exploration-exploitation strategy
(e.g., epsilon-greedy)
        action = choose_action(state, Q)


# Take action and receive reward
        next_state, reward = take_action(state, action)


# Update Q-value based on Bellman equation (simplified)
        Q[state, action] = Q[state, action] + learning_rate *
(reward + discount_factor * max(Q[next_state, :]))
        state = next_state
```

Benefits of Q-Learning:

1. Easy to understand and implement for beginners in

RL.

2. Works well for problems with a discrete set of states and actions.

Challenges of Q-Learning:

1. The Q-table can become very large for complex coding environments with many possible states and actions.

2. Exploration vs. exploitation balance can be tricky to manage. Too much exploration can slow down learning, while too much exploitation can prevent the agent from discovering potentially better actions.

2.2 Deep Q-Networks (DQN): Leveraging Deep Learning for Complex Tasks

Q-Learning shines for simple environments. However, real-world coding tasks often involve complex situations with numerous states and actions. Here's where Deep Q-Networks (DQN) comes in.

DQN builds upon Q-Learning by introducing a deep neural network to approximate the Q-values. This network can handle a vast number of states and actions, making it suitable for complex coding problems.

Here's the gist of DQN:

Experience Replay: DQN stores past experiences (state, action, reward, next state) in a replay memory. This allows the agent to learn from a broader set of experiences, not just the most recent ones.

Neural Network Architecture: The DQN uses a convolutional neural network (CNN) or a recurrent neural network (RNN) to analyze the environment and predict Q-values for all possible actions in a given state. CNNs are well-suited for tasks where the spatial relationship between code elements matters (e.g., code structure). RNNs can handle sequential data, useful for tasks involving code generation or debugging where order matters.

Benefits of DQN:

1. Handles complex coding environments with numerous

states and actions.

2. Learn from a diverse set of experiences through experience replay.

Challenges of DQN:

1. Requires more computational resources compared to Q-Learning due to the deep neural network.
2. Tuning the hyperparameters (learning rate, network architecture) of the DQN can be crucial for optimal performance.

Code Snippet (Conceptual - Python libraries like TensorFlow are needed for actual implementation):

python

```python
# Define experience replay memory
memory = ReplayMemory(capacity)
```

CHAPTER 3

SETTING UP YOUR RL ENVIRONMENT FOR CODING

This chapter equips you with the tools and techniques to set up your RL environment specifically for coding tasks.

3.1 Choosing the Right Tools and Frameworks: OpenAI Gym, TensorFlow, etc.

Just like any programmer needs the right tools for the job, RL for coding requires specific frameworks and libraries. Here are some popular choices:

OpenAI Gym: This is a widely used toolkit for developing and testing RL agents. It provides a standardized interface for defining environments and interacting with them. Imagine a virtual gym where you can train your coding RL agent on various coding challenges.

TensorFlow or PyTorch: These are powerful deep learning libraries that can be used to implement various RL algorithms, including DQN. They offer functionalities for building and training neural networks, a crucial component of DQN for complex coding tasks.

Choosing the right tools depends on your project's complexity and your familiarity with specific libraries.

Here's a general guideline:

1. For simpler coding tasks and getting started with RL, OpenAI Gym with a basic RL library might suffice.

2. For complex tasks involving deep learning and neural networks, consider using TensorFlow or PyTorch alongside OpenAI Gym.

Additional Libraries:

Scikit-learn: This library provides useful tools for data manipulation and preprocessing, often necessary for preparing your coding data for the RL agent.

Code Analysis Libraries: Depending on your specific coding environment, you might leverage libraries for parsing and analyzing code structure (e.g., AST in Python).

Real-life Example: Let's say you want to train an RL agent to suggest code completions in Python. You could use OpenAI Gym to define a custom environment where the state represents the current line of code being written, and the actions could be suggesting different code snippets for completion. TensorFlow could then be used to implement a DQN that learns from past suggestions and rewards (e.g., +1 for completing the code correctly, -1 for suggesting an incorrect completion).

3.2 Defining the Coding Task as an RL Problem: State Representation, Actions, and Rewards

Before training your RL agent, you need to translate your coding task into the language of RL.

Here are the key elements to define:

State Representation: This encompasses the information the agent receives about the current coding situation. It could be the current line of code, the surrounding code block, or even information about the overall project structure. Imagine providing a snapshot of the coding challenge to your agent.

Actions: These are the options the agent can choose from to manipulate the coding environment. This could be suggesting code completions, proposing code refactoring options, or even generating entire code snippets. Think of these as the tools your agent has to solve the coding problem.

Rewards: As mentioned earlier, rewards are crucial for guiding the agent's learning. In a coding context, rewards could be assigned for positive outcomes like writing correct and efficient code. Penalties (negative rewards) could be given for suggesting incorrect completions or generating buggy code. Rewards act as feedback mechanisms for the agent.

Real-life Example

In our code completion example, the state representation could be the current line of code being written along with the previous few lines for context. The actions could be suggesting different Python keywords or function calls to complete the line. The reward could be +1 if the suggested completion compiles and runs correctly, and -1 if it leads to an error.

Code Snippet (Python - OpenAI Gym example - simplified):

python

```python
class CodeCompletionEnv(gym.Env):
    def __init__(self):
        # Define state representation (e.g., current line of code)
        # Define action space (e.g., list of possible code completions)
        pass

    def reset(self):
        # Reset the coding environment (e.g., load a new code snippet)
        return state

    def step(self, action):
        # Take action (e.g., suggest code completion)
        # Update state and calculate reward based on the outcome
        return next_state, reward, done, info
```

Remember, defining these elements effectively is vital for the success of your RL agent. Carefully consider what information the agent needs (state), what actions it can take, and how to provide meaningful rewards to guide its learning process.

3.3 Training Your RL Agent: Hyperparameter Tuning and Monitoring Performance

Once you've defined your RL environment, it's time to train your agent! Here's what to keep in mind:

Here are some key things to keep in mind when training your RL agent after defining your RL environment:

Hyperparameter Tuning: RL algorithms often have various hyperparameters that significantly impact their performance. These can include:

Learning Rate: This controls how quickly the agent updates its knowledge based on new experiences. A high learning rate can lead to instability and poor convergence, while a low learning rate can make training very slow.

Discount Factor: This parameter determines how much weight the agent places on future rewards compared to immediate ones. A high discount factor encourages the agent to consider long-term consequences of its actions, while a low discount factor prioritizes immediate rewards.

Exploration vs. Exploitation: As discussed earlier, there's a balance between exploration (trying new actions) and exploitation (focusing on actions with proven rewards). You might need to adjust exploration strategies (e.g., epsilon-greedy) during training to ensure the agent explores sufficiently while also capitalizing on its learned knowledge.

Monitoring Performance: It's crucial to track your agent's performance during training. Here are some useful metrics:

Episode Reward: This measures the average reward achieved per training episode (a complete interaction between the agent and the environment until a goal is reached or a stopping condition is met). Observing the trend in episode reward over time indicates if the agent is learning and improving.

Loss Function: Depending on the specific RL algorithm, you might monitor the loss function, which signifies the discrepancy between the agent's predictions and the actual rewards. A decreasing loss function suggests the agent is making better predictions over time.

Visualization: Visualizing the agent's behavior in the

environment can be insightful. This could involve logging code snippets it generates or suggested code refactorings. Analyzing these outputs can help identify areas for improvement or potential biases in the training data.

Computational Resources: Training RL agents, especially with deep learning techniques, can be computationally expensive. Consider factors like the complexity of your environment, the chosen RL algorithm, and the available hardware resources (CPU, GPU) when planning your training runs.

Overfitting and Generalization: Just like with any machine learning model, there's a risk of overfitting, where the agent performs well on the specific training data but fails to generalize to unseen coding challenges. Techniques like using a validation set and dropout regularization (in neural network architectures) can help mitigate overfitting and improve the agent's ability to handle new coding scenarios.

By carefully considering these aspects and iteratively refining your environment definition, hyperparameter tuning, and training process, you can effectively train your RL agent to become a valuable assistant in your coding endeavors.

CHAPTER 4

PUTTING IT ALL TOGETHER: CODING WITH YOUR RL AGENT

Chapter 3 equipped you with the knowledge to set up your RL environment for coding tasks. Now, it's time to unleash the power of your trained agent and see it in action! This chapter explores how to integrate your RL agent into your coding workflow and leverage its capabilities for various tasks.

4.1 Code Completion with RL

Imagine having an intelligent assistant that suggests code completions as you type. This can be a reality with your trained RL agent! Here's how to achieve it:

Integration with Code Editor: There are various ways to integrate your RL agent with your preferred code editor. You can develop a custom plugin that communicates with the agent in real-time. The editor would send the current line of code (state) to the agent, and the agent would respond with suggested completions (actions).

Real-time Decision Making: For real-time code completion, efficiency is crucial. Techniques like beam search can be employed to identify a shortlist of high-probability code completions without exploring the entire action space exhaustively.

Real-life Example:

Let's revisit our code completion example from Chapter 3. Your trained RL agent, constantly monitoring your coding activity, would receive the current line of code you're writing. Based on its knowledge of Python syntax and the context of the surrounding code, it would recommend relevant keywords, function calls, or code snippets to complete the line efficiently.

Code Snippet (Python - Conceptual - Integration with code editor would require specific libraries depending on the editor):

python

```
# Simplified example to illustrate communication with the
agent
   def suggest_completion(current_line):
      state = prepare_state(current_line)  # Convert line to
agent- understandable format
      action = agent.choose_action(state)
         return translate_action(action)   # Convert action to
human-readable suggestion
```

4.2 Code Refactoring with RL

Beyond code completion, your RL agent can assist with code refactoring tasks. Here's the approach:

State Representation for Refactoring: The state representation for code refactoring might encompass the entire code block or function being refactored. Additionally, code quality metrics (e.g., code complexity) could be incorporated to guide the agent.

Action Space for Refactoring: The actions could involve suggesting different refactoring techniques like variable renaming, function extraction, or code inlining. The agent would choose actions that improve code readability, maintainability, or performance based on the reward function.

Real-life Example:

Your RL agent, analyzing a complex function in your code, might propose refactoring it into smaller, more manageable functions. This could improve code readability and potentially enhance performance.

Note: Refactoring with RL is an active research area. While promising, current techniques might not handle all refactoring scenarios perfectly. Human expertise is still crucial for reviewing and approving suggested refactoring actions from the agent.

4.3 Code Generation with RL

RL can be used not only for code completion and refactoring but also for generating entirely new code snippets. Here's a glimpse into this advanced application:

Sequence-to-Sequence Learning: This deep learning

approach is well-suited for code generation tasks. The agent learns to map an initial code sequence (state) to a desired output sequence (generated code).

Challenges and Considerations: Generating entire code functionalities with RL is challenging. It requires a vast amount of training data and careful design of the reward function to ensure the generated code is not only syntactically correct but also functionally sound. Additionally, safety considerations are crucial when dealing with code generation, as errors can have real-world consequences.

Real-life Example (Limited Scope):

Imagine an RL agent trained on a large dataset of code snippets for simple mathematical functions. It could then be used to generate basic code for calculating things like area, volume, or distance based on user input. However, for complex functionalities, human intervention and review would likely still be necessary.

Code Snippet (Conceptual - High-level overview due to complexity):

python

This is a high-level representation due to the complexity of sequence-to-sequence models with RL

```
model = build_seq2seq_model(state_size, action_size)
generated_code = model.generate(initial_code_sequence)
```

Remember, RL-powered code generation is a rapidly evolving field. As research progresses, we can expect more sophisticated techniques and applications to emerge in the future.

4.4 Beyond the Code: Soft Skills for the RL Coder

While RL can automate many coding tasks, some aspects require strong human skills:

Problem Decomposition: Breaking down complex coding problems into smaller, manageable tasks suitable for your RL agent is crucial. This involves understanding the core functionalities and identifying areas where the agent's capabilities can be effectively applied.

Data Curation and Quality: The performance of your RL agent hinges on the quality of data it's trained on. You'll need to curate well-structured and relevant coding data for your specific use case. This might involve collecting code samples, ensuring they are functional and error-free, and potentially labeling them with desired outcomes.

Evaluation and Human Oversight: Even with a well-trained RL agent, human evaluation and oversight remain essential. It's crucial to assess the agent's outputs (suggested completions, refactoring proposals, or generated code) and identify any errors or shortcomings. Human judgment is necessary to ensure the final code meets coding standards, functionality requirements, and safety considerations.

Understanding RL Limitations: While RL is a powerful tool, it's not a silver bullet. It's essential to understand the limitations of RL for coding tasks. The agent might struggle with highly creative coding tasks, edge cases, or situations requiring complex logic beyond its learned patterns.

Continuous Learning and Improvement: As you use your RL agent in real-world coding scenarios, you'll gain valuable insights into its strengths and weaknesses. Continuously improving your agent involves iteratively refining the training data, adjusting hyperparameters, and potentially retraining the agent to enhance its performance over time.

RL in coding is a collaborative effort between humans and machines. By leveraging the automation power of RL while applying your problem-solving, data analysis, and critical thinking skills, you can unlock a new level of efficiency and creativity in your coding endeavors.

CHAPTER 5

OPTIMIZING CODE PERFORMANCE WITH RL

RL can be used to optimize the performance of your code.

5.1 Algorithm Selection: Choosing the Right RL Technique for Performance Optimization

Not all RL algorithms are created equal. When optimizing code performance, the choice of algorithm depends on the specific challenge:

1. For discrete optimization problems (e.g., selecting the most efficient sorting algorithm for a specific dataset size), Q-Learning or Policy Gradient methods might be suitable.
2. For continuous optimization problems (e.g., fine-tuning hyperparameters of a machine learning model), techniques like Deep Deterministic Policy Gradient (DDPG) can be effective.

Real-life Example:

Imagine you have a complex sorting algorithm in your code. You could train an RL agent to experiment with different sorting algorithms (actions) on various datasets (states) and choose the one that consistently delivers the fastest execution time (reward).

5.2 Learning Efficient Data Structures: Optimizing Data Access Patterns

The choice of data structures significantly impacts code performance. RL can be used to:

Learn Optimal Data Structures: An RL agent could be trained to analyze code and data usage patterns. Based on this analysis, it could suggest switching to a more efficient data structure (e.g., using a hash table instead of a linear search) to improve code performance.

Real-life Example:

Let's say your code iterates through a large list to find specific elements. An RL agent, after analyzing the access patterns, might recommend using a set instead, which offers faster lookups for element existence.

5.3 Algorithm Parameter Tuning: Using RL to Find Optimal Algorithmic Parameters

Many algorithms have configurable parameters that affect their performance. RL can be employed to:

Tune Hyperparameters: An RL agent could explore different hyperparameter settings (actions) for an algorithm within a defined range. By evaluating the resulting performance (reward), the agent can learn to identify the optimal configuration for a specific scenario.

Real-life Example:

Consider a machine learning model with hyperparameters like learning rate and number of training epochs. An RL agent could experiment with different combinations and choose the configuration that leads to the highest model accuracy (reward).

Code Snippet (Conceptual - High-level overview due to

complexity):

python

```
# This is a high-level representation due to the complexity
of hyperparameter tuning with RL
def                       train_with_rl_tuning(algorithm,
hyperparameter_ranges):
    agent = RL_agent(action_space=hyperparameter_ranges)
    # Train the agent to explore hyperparameter space and
maximize reward (performance metric)
    agent.train(...)
    return agent.get_best_hyperparameters()
```

5.4 Resource Management: Learning to Allocate Resources Efficiently Within Code

Code execution often involves managing resources like memory or network bandwidth. RL can be employed for:

Resource Allocation: An RL agent could learn to dynamically allocate resources (actions) based on the code's current execution state. This could involve strategies like memory caching or throttling network requests to optimize resource usage.

Real-life Example:

Imagine a web application handling multiple user requests. An RL agent could monitor resource usage and dynamically adjust memory allocation between different user sessions (actions) to ensure optimal application performance.

Optimizing code performance with RL is an active research area. While promising, current techniques might require careful problem formulation and experimentation to achieve optimal results. However, RL offers exciting possibilities for building high-performing and resource-efficient code in the future.

CHAPTER 6

BUILDING SELF-LEARNING AI ASSISTANTS FOR CODERS

Let's delve into the future of coding with intelligent AI assistants powered by RL.

6.1 Context-Aware Code Completion: Suggesting Code Based on Project and User Intent

Imagine a code completion tool that understands the context of your project and your coding intent. This is the power of RL-driven code completion:

Beyond Basic Completions: Current code completion tools often suggest keywords or function names based on the current line of code. RL assistants can go further, considering the broader project structure, surrounding code blocks, and even your past coding habits.

Learning from Project Context: The RL agent would be trained on various coding projects and learn to identify coding patterns and conventions specific to different domains (e.g., web development vs. machine learning). This context awareness would enable it to suggest completions that not only fit syntactically but also align with the project's purpose.

Real-life Example (Future Scenario):

As you're building a web application and writing code for a user login functionality, your RL assistant, understanding the context, might not only suggest completions for username and password input fields but also recommend relevant libraries for handling user authentication securely.

6.2 Intelligent Debugging Assistants: Leveraging RL to Diagnose and Resolve Errors

Debugging can be a time-consuming task. RL can assist you in this process:

Identifying Potential Bugs: The RL agent, trained on a vast dataset of code with known bugs, could analyze your code and highlight areas with a high probability of causing errors. This would help you prioritize your debugging efforts.

Suggesting Code Fixes: Beyond identifying bugs, RL assistants might even propose potential code fixes (actions) based on their learned patterns from successful bug fixes in similar code scenarios. This can significantly accelerate the debugging process.

Real-life Example (Future Scenario):

Encountering an error in your code related to handling user input validation, your RL assistant might not only pinpoint the line causing the issue but also suggest a fix involving adding appropriate data type checks to prevent the error from occurring again.

Note: It's important to remember that RL-powered debugging assistants are still under development. While they can be valuable tools, human expertise remains crucial for complex debugging scenarios and critical decision-making.

6.3 Personalized Coding Recommendations: Suggesting Best Practices and Libraries

Every coder strives to write clean, efficient, and

maintainable code. RL assistants can help you achieve this by:

Recommending Best Practices: The RL agent, having learned from a codebase of well-written and efficient code, could suggest improvements to your code structure, variable naming conventions, or coding style. This would help you adhere to best practices and improve code readability.

Context-Aware Library Suggestions: For specific coding tasks, the RL assistant could recommend relevant libraries or frameworks based on the project requirements and the code context. This can save you time searching for appropriate tools and libraries.

Real-life Example (Future Scenario):

While working on data analysis code, your RL assistant might analyze your approach and suggest using a specific library like Pandas for efficient data manipulation tasks, along with code examples demonstrating how to integrate the library effectively.

6.4 Collaborative Coding with AI Agents: Automating Mundane Tasks and Error Checking

Imagine an AI agent working alongside you, automating repetitive tasks and catching potential errors before they become problems:

Automating Repetitive Tasks: Tedious tasks like writing boilerplate code or basic unit tests could be handled by the RL agent, freeing you to focus on the more creative and strategic aspects of coding.

Real-time Error Checking: As you write code, the RL agent could continuously analyze your work and highlight potential syntax errors, logical inconsistencies, or inefficiencies in your code structure. This real-time feedback can help you write cleaner and more robust code.

Real-life Example (Future Scenario):

While working on a complex function, the RL agent might not only automate generating the basic function structure but also continuously check your code for potential errors like missing semicolons or incorrect function call arguments, providing instant feedback to help you avoid mistakes.

RL-powered coding assistants are here to augment your coding skills, not replace them. By leveraging their capabilities for context-aware suggestions, intelligent debugging assistance, and real-time error checking, you can become a more efficient and productive coder.

CHAPTER 7

Integrating RL with Existing Development Tools

RL can be integrated with the tools you already use to streamline your development workflow.

7.1 Plugin Development for IDEs: Enhancing Code Editors with RL Functionality

Imagine your favorite code editor equipped with an RL-powered plugin that anticipates your needs and assists you in real-time. Here's what this integration could look like:

Context-Aware Code Completion with RL: Leveraging RL, the plugin could analyze your current code, project structure, and even your coding style to suggest highly relevant code completions that go beyond basic syntax suggestions.

Real-time Error Prevention: The plugin could continuously monitor your code as you type, identifying potential syntax errors, logical inconsistencies, or inefficiencies. This real-time feedback can help you prevent errors before they occur.

Real-life Example (Simplified and Conceptual):

Imagine an RL-powered plugin for Python development. As you start writing a function to calculate the area of a circle, the plugin would not only suggest the "pi" constant but also anticipate your need for the formula (pi * radius**2) and provide context-aware completions as you progress. Additionally, it might highlight potential errors like typos or incorrect function calls, preventing issues before you run the code.

Note: Developing RL plugins for IDEs requires expertise in both RL and the specific IDE's plugin development environment. Open-source libraries and frameworks can provide a foundation for building such plugins.

7.2 Continuous Integration and Delivery (CI/CD) with RL: Automating Testing and Deployment

CI/CD pipelines automate the software development

process, including testing and deployment. RL can be integrated into this pipeline to:

Adaptive Testing Strategies: An RL agent could analyze code changes and historical testing data to prioritize and optimize test execution. This could involve focusing on areas with a higher likelihood of introducing bugs based on the changes made.

Predictive Deployment Rollouts: The RL agent could learn from past deployment patterns and predict potential issues during a new deployment. This can help identify scenarios where a rollback might be necessary, ensuring smoother deployment processes.

Real-life Example (Simplified and Conceptual):

Imagine a CI/CD pipeline that includes unit tests for your code. The RL agent, analyzing your code changes, might prioritize running tests related to the modified sections and de-prioritize tests for unchanged functionalities. This can save time during the testing phase. Additionally, based on historical deployment data, the agent might predict a higher chance of issues in a specific environment, prompting a slower rollout or additional checks before deploying to production.

Note: Integrating RL with CI/CD pipelines is an emerging area. Security and reliability considerations are crucial when deploying RL-powered automation within CI/CD workflows.

7.3 Version Control with RL: Learning Optimal Code Merging Strategies

Version control systems (VCS) like Git help manage code changes and collaboration. RL can potentially assist with:

Conflict Resolution During Merging: Merging code branches can sometimes lead to conflicts. An RL agent, trained on various merging scenarios, could suggest optimal merge strategies to resolve conflicts efficiently while minimizing the risk of introducing errors.

Predicting Merge Issues: The RL agent could analyze code changes from different branches and predict potential conflicts that might arise during merging. This proactive approach can help developers identify and address issues before they become roadblocks.

Real-life Example (Simplified and Conceptual):

Imagine you're working on a feature branch and merging your changes with the main codebase. The RL agent, analyzing both codebases, might highlight potential conflicts due to changes in the same code sections and suggest appropriate merge strategies to handle these conflicts effectively. Additionally, it might warn you about areas with a high likelihood of merge issues, allowing you to proactively address them before merging.

Using RL for VCS automation is an active research area. Human expertise remains essential for reviewing and approving merge suggestions from RL agents in critical scenarios.

7.4 Building Scalable RL-Powered Coding Workflows

Integrating RL with various development tools can create powerful coding workflows. Here are key considerations:

Modular Design: When developing RL-powered

functionalities for your coding environment, strive for a modular design approach. This involves breaking down your RL applications into reusable modules for different tasks, such as code completion, error checking, test case generation, or refactoring suggestions. Each module can be trained on specific datasets and optimized for its individual purpose.

Benefits of Modular Design:

Flexibility and Reusability: Modular components can be easily integrated with various development tools and workflows. You can combine different modules to create a comprehensive RL-powered coding assistant.

Maintainability and Updatability: As RL techniques and your coding needs evolve, individual modules can be updated or replaced without affecting the entire system. This promotes long-term maintainability of your RL-powered coding environment.

Data Management and Security: The performance of RL agents heavily relies on the quality and relevance of the training data. Here's how to ensure effective data management and security for your RL-powered coding workflows:

Data Collection Strategies: Develop strategies to collect high-quality code data for training your RL agents. This could involve using code repositories from open-source projects (with proper licensing considerations), anonymized internal codebases, or synthetically generated code examples.

Data Storage and Security: Implement secure data storage solutions to house your code data. This might involve using version control systems or secure cloud storage platforms. Ensure proper access controls and encryption mechanisms are in place to protect sensitive information within the code.

Data Preprocessing and Cleaning: Before feeding data into your RL models, it's crucial to preprocess and clean it. This might involve removing irrelevant information, handling inconsistencies, and ensuring data quality to prevent training biases in your RL agents.

Monitoring and Human Oversight: It's essential to continuously monitor the performance of your RL-powered tools within your development workflow. Here's how to ensure effective monitoring and maintain human control:

Performance Metrics: Establish clear performance metrics to track the effectiveness of your RL-powered tools. This could involve metrics like accuracy of code suggestions, reduction in errors detected during testing, or improvement in developer productivity.

Human-in-the-Loop Approach: While RL offers automation capabilities, human oversight remains crucial, especially in critical decision-making processes. Developers should review and approve suggestions or recommendations provided by RL agents before integrating them into the final codebase. This ensures that the overall quality, security, and maintainability of the code are upheld.

Feedback Mechanisms: Implement feedback mechanisms for developers to provide feedback on the performance of RL-powered tools. This feedback can be used to continuously improve the training data, refine the RL models, and enhance the overall experience for users.

Following these considerations, you can build scalable and reliable RL-powered coding workflows that integrate seamlessly with your existing development tools. Remember, RL is here to augment your coding skills, not replace them. Leverage the power of RL to automate repetitive tasks, improve code quality, and streamline your development process, allowing you to focus on the creative and strategic aspects of coding.

CHAPTER 8

ETHICAL CONSIDERATIONS AND CHALLENGES OF RL IN CODING

While RL offers exciting possibilities for enhancing coding efficiency and productivity, it's crucial to address the ethical considerations and challenges that come with this technology. As with any powerful tool, ensuring responsible development and use of RL in coding is paramount.

8.1 Bias in Training Data: Mitigating Bias in RL Models for Fair and Equitable Coding Tools

The Challenge:

RL models learn from the data they are trained on. If the training data contains biases, these biases can be reflected in the recommendations and suggestions provided by the RL-powered coding tools. For instance, an RL model trained on codebases with a historical gender imbalance in authorship might perpetuate these biases by favoring coding styles or libraries more commonly used by one gender group.

Consequences of Bias:

Unfair and Unequal Outcomes: Biased RL tools could disadvantage certain coders, hindering their productivity and creativity.

Reinforcing Existing Biases: Perpetuating biases in the coding ecosystem could further limit diversity and inclusion within the field.

Mitigating Bias:

Curated Training Data: When creating training data for RL models used in coding tools, it's essential to ensure diversity and representativeness. This might involve using code from various sources, including projects from underrepresented groups in tech.

Debiasing Techniques: Techniques like data augmentation and fairness-aware model training algorithms can help reduce bias in RL models for coding tasks.

8.2 Explainability and Transparency: Understanding How RL Models Make Coding Decisions

The Challenge:

The inner workings of some RL algorithms can be complex, making it difficult to understand how they arrive at their recommendations or suggestions for coders. This lack of transparency can be problematic, especially when dealing with critical coding decisions.

Why Explainability Matters:

Trust and Confidence: Coders need to trust the suggestions provided by RL tools. Explainability helps build trust by allowing developers to understand the rationale behind the recommendations.

Debugging and Improvement: Understanding how RL models reach their decisions is crucial for debugging potential issues and identifying areas where the models can be improved.

Enhancing Explainability:

Interpretable RL Algorithms: Research in RL is exploring algorithms that are inherently more interpretable, allowing for easier understanding of their decision-making processes.

Visualization Techniques: Developing visualization tools can help explain how RL models analyze code and arrive at their suggestions.

8.3 Security and Safety Concerns: Preventing Malicious Use of RL-Generated Code

The Challenge:

As RL advances, the possibility of using it to generate malicious code becomes a concern. Attackers could potentially train RL models to create code with vulnerabilities or backdoors that compromise systems.

Security Considerations:

Code Security Audits: Any code generated or suggested by RL tools, especially for critical applications, should undergo thorough security audits to identify and mitigate potential vulnerabilities.

Safe Training Data and Environments: It's crucial to ensure that the training data for RL models used in coding tools is secure and free from malicious code examples. Additionally, implementing secure training environments can help prevent manipulation of the training process.

8.4 The Future of Work: Impact of RL on Coding Jobs and Skillsets

The Potential Impact:

The rise of RL-powered coding tools might raise concerns about job displacement for coders. However, RL is more likely to augment human capabilities than replace them entirely.

The Evolving Role of Coders:

Focus on Creativity and Strategy: With RL handling repetitive tasks, coders can focus on the creative aspects of programming, like designing algorithms, solving complex problems, and building innovative applications.

New Skillsets: As RL integration with coding tools

progresses, coders might need to develop new skillsets, such as understanding RL principles, working with RL-powered tools, and interpreting their recommendations effectively.

The Importance of Human Expertise:

Despite the capabilities of RL, human expertise remains essential in the coding field.

Critical Thinking and Decision-Making: Coders will still be responsible for making critical decisions about code architecture, design choices, and the overall direction of a project. RL can provide valuable suggestions, but human judgment remains crucial.

Adaptability and Problem-Solving: The ability to adapt to new technologies, solve unforeseen problems, and think creatively will continue to be highly sought-after skills for coders in the age of RL-powered coding tools.

By acknowledging and addressing the ethical considerations and challenges associated with RL in coding, we can ensure the responsible development and use of this technology. RL has the potential to revolutionize coding practices, but it's up to us to harness its power for good and promote a more efficient, inclusive, and secure coding future.

CHAPTER 9

ADVANCED TECHNIQUES AND RESEARCH FRONTIERS IN RL FOR CODERS

Let's delve into the exciting world of cutting-edge research areas pushing the boundaries of RL for coders.

9.1 Hierarchical Reinforcement Learning: Breaking Down Complex Coding Tasks

The Challenge:

Many real-world coding tasks are complex and involve multiple subtasks. Traditional RL approaches might struggle to handle such situations efficiently.

Hierarchical RL to the Rescue:

Hierarchical RL decomposes complex tasks into smaller, more manageable subtasks. The RL agent learns to perform these subtasks in a coordinated manner to achieve the overall goal. This hierarchical approach allows for more efficient learning and decision-making for complex coding problems.

Real-life Example (Simplified and Conceptual):

Imagine training an RL agent to write a complex function that analyzes user data and generates custom reports. Using hierarchical RL, the agent could first learn subtasks like data cleaning, data filtering, and data visualization. Then, it would learn how to combine these subtasks in the correct sequence to achieve the final goal of report generation.

Benefits of Hierarchical RL:

Improved Efficiency: By breaking down complex tasks, hierarchical RL allows the agent to focus on learning each subtask efficiently.

Better Generalizability: The learned subtasks can be potentially reused in different coding contexts, improving the overall adaptability of the RL agent.

9.2 Multi-Agent Reinforcement Learning: Collaboration Between Coders and RL Agents

The Challenge:

Many coding projects involve collaboration between multiple developers. Traditional RL often focuses on single-agent scenarios.

Multi-Agent RL for Teamwork:

Multi-agent RL (MARL) allows multiple RL agents to learn and collaborate with each other. This opens doors for interesting possibilities in coding, where human coders and RL agents can work together.

Real-life Example (Simplified and Conceptual):

Imagine a scenario where an RL agent assists a coder in building a multi-player game. The RL agent could learn aspects of the game AI, while the human coder focuses on game mechanics and user interface design. Through MARL, both the coder and the agent could learn from each other and adapt their strategies to create a more engaging game experience.

Challenges and Considerations of MARL:

Coordination and Communication: Developing effective communication and coordination mechanisms between human coders and RL agents is crucial for successful collaboration in a MARL setting.

Reward Sharing and Alignment: Designing reward structures that incentivize both the RL agent and the human coder to work towards a common goal is an important aspect of MARL for coding tasks.

9.3 Transfer Learning: Leveraging Pre-Trained RL Models for Faster Learning

The Challenge:

Training RL models from scratch can be time-consuming and resource-intensive.

Transfer Learning for a Head Start:

Transfer learning involves leveraging knowledge gained from a pre-trained RL model on a related task and applying it to a new task. This can significantly reduce the time and resources required to train an RL agent for a specific coding problem.

Real-life Example (Simplified and Conceptual):

Imagine you've already trained an RL agent to identify common coding bugs in web applications. Using transfer learning, you could leverage this pre-trained model to develop a new RL agent that focuses on identifying security vulnerabilities in web applications. The pre-trained model's knowledge of code analysis and bug identification can be a valuable starting point for the new agent.

Benefits of Transfer Learning:

Faster Training Times: By leveraging pre-trained models, coders can develop RL-powered tools more quickly and efficiently.

Improved Performance: Transfer learning can help RL agents achieve better performance on new tasks by building upon existing knowledge.

9.4 Continuous Learning: Adapting RL Models to Evolving Coding Environments

The Challenge:

The world of coding is constantly evolving with new languages, frameworks, and best practices emerging. RL models need to adapt to these changes to remain effective.

Continuous Learning for Adaptability:

Continuous learning algorithms allow RL models to continuously learn and update their knowledge based on new experiences and data. This ensures that the models remain relevant and effective even as coding practices evolve.

Real-life Example (Simplified and Conceptual):

Imagine an RL-powered code completion tool trained on a dataset of Python code. With the emergence of a new popular Python library, the continuous learning algorithm could allow the RL model to adapt and learn how to suggest code completions that utilize the functionalities of this new library.

Challenges of Continuous Learning

Data Drift: As coding practices evolve, the data used to train the RL model might become outdated. Mitigating data drift is crucial for effective continuous learning.

Stability and Performance: Balancing continuous learning with maintaining the stability

Challenges of Continuous Learning (continued):

Balancing continuous learning with maintaining the stability and performance of the RL model is an ongoing area of research. Techniques like experience replay with prioritized sampling can help ensure the model retains valuable knowledge from past experiences while incorporating new information effectively.

Benefits of Continuous Learning:

Improved Long-Term Performance: By continuously adapting, RL models can maintain their effectiveness in real-world coding scenarios that are constantly changing.

Reduced Need for Retraining: Continuous learning algorithms can reduce the need for frequent retraining of RL models as new coding practices emerge.

The Future of RL for Coders

The research frontiers explored in this chapter represent the leading edge of RL for coders. As these techniques mature and become more accessible, we can expect even more powerful and versatile RL-powered tools to emerge, transforming the coding landscape. Here are some exciting possibilities for the future:

Personalized RL Assistants: RL agents that can tailor their suggestions and recommendations to a coder's specific style, preferences, and project requirements.

Explainable and Interpretable RL: Advancements in explainable RL will make it easier for coders to understand the decision-making processes behind RL suggestions, fostering trust and collaboration.

Democratization of RL for Coders: With user-friendly tools and frameworks, even coders with limited RL expertise will be able to leverage the power of RL to enhance their workflows.

Embracing these advancements and fostering a responsible approach to RL development, we can unlock a future where RL empowers coders to be more efficient, productive, and creative in their endeavors.

CHAPTER 10

CONCLUSION AND FUTURE OUTLOOK

As we conclude our exploration of reinforcement learning (RL) for coders, let's recap the exciting possibilities and transformative potential of this technology, while also acknowledging the ongoing journey of development and responsible implementation.

10.1 The Future of RL-Powered Coding Tools and Assistants

The future of coding holds immense promise with the integration of RL. Here's a glimpse of what we can expect:

More Sophisticated RL Algorithms: Advancements in RL research will lead to the development of even more powerful and versatile algorithms specifically tailored for coding tasks. This will enable RL-powered tools to handle a wider range of coding challenges with greater efficiency and accuracy.

Seamless Integration with Existing Environments: RL functionalities will become seamlessly integrated into popular

IDEs, code editors, and CI/CD pipelines. This will make RL-powered coding assistants readily available to coders within their existing workflows, minimizing disruption and maximizing adoption.

Focus on Explainability and Trust: As explainable RL techniques mature, RL-powered tools will become more transparent in their decision-making processes. This will build trust with coders and allow them to understand the rationale behind suggestions and recommendations provided by RL assistants.

Real-life Example (Simplified and Conceptual):

Imagine a future where your favorite code editor comes equipped with an RL-powered assistant that can not only suggest code completions but also explain why those suggestions are relevant in the context of your current code and project goals. Additionally, the assistant might highlight potential issues or inefficiencies in your code and suggest alternative approaches based on its learned understanding of best practices and coding patterns.

10.2 The Role of Human Expertise in the Age of AI-Driven Programming

While RL offers significant automation capabilities, human expertise remains irreplaceable in the coding profession:

Critical Thinking and Decision-Making: The ability to analyze problems, make critical decisions about code architecture, and choose the right tools and techniques will continue to be a cornerstone of successful coding. RL can provide valuable insights and suggestions, but human judgment will always be essential.

Creativity and Innovation: The ability to think outside the box, come up with novel solutions, and design innovative applications will remain a key differentiator for human coders in the age of RL. RL excels at automating repetitive tasks and learning from existing codebases, but it cannot replicate human creativity.

The Future of the Human-AI Partnership:

The future of coding lies in a synergistic partnership between human and AI capabilities. RL-powered tools will augment human coders by automating repetitive tasks, identifying potential issues, and suggesting optimizations. However, human coders will continue to be the driving force behind innovation, creativity, and the application of code to solve real-world problems.

10.3 Embracing the Potential of RL for a More Efficient and Creative Coding Experience

By embracing RL, coders can unlock a new level of efficiency and productivity:

Reduced Time Spent on Mundane Tasks: RL can automate repetitive coding tasks like code completion, unit test generation, and code refactoring. This frees up valuable time for coders to focus on the more creative and strategic aspects of programming.

Improved Code Quality and Maintainability: RL-powered tools can help identify potential coding errors and suggest improvements to code structure and maintainability. This leads to a higher overall code quality and reduces the time spent on debugging and fixing issues later in the development process.

Exploration of New Possibilities: With RL handling routine tasks, coders can experiment with new technologies and approaches more readily. This fosters innovation and opens doors to the creation of more complex and powerful applications.

A More Fulfilling Coding Journey:

By leveraging the power of RL, coders can streamline their workflows, reduce the tedium of repetitive tasks, and focus on the aspects of programming that they find most fulfilling: problem-solving, innovation, and creating software that makes a difference.

10.4 Resources for Further Learning and Exploration in RL for Coders

The field of RL for coders is rapidly evolving. Here are some resources to help you stay updated and continue your exploration:

Online Courses and Tutorials:
Platforms: Platforms like Coursera, Udacity, and edX offer

courses on Reinforcement Learning with sections or specializations focused on coding applications.

Examples: Courses like "Introduction to Reinforcement Learning for Coders" or "Building Your First RL-Powered Coding Assistant" can provide a practical introduction to the field.

Open-Source Libraries and Frameworks:

Libraries: Open-source libraries like OpenAI Gym, Stable Baselines3, and RLlib provide building blocks for developing RL agents for coding tasks.

Frameworks: Frameworks like Ray RLlib or Coach from Uber offer higher-level functionalities to simplify the process of building and deploying RL-powered coding tools.

Communities: Getting involved in online communities around these libraries and frameworks allows you to connect with other developers interested in RL for coding, share knowledge, and learn from each other's experiences.

Research Papers and Articles:

Publications: Top conferences in AI, such as NeurIPS (Neural Information Processing Systems) and ICLR (International Conference on Learning Representations), often publish research papers on advancements in RL for coding tasks.

Websites: Tech blogs and websites like Machine Learning Mastery, The Gradient, and Towards Data Science frequently publish articles that explore the latest trends and applications of RL in coding.

The field of RL for coders is constantly evolving. By staying curious, exploring the available resources, and actively participating in the learning community, you can equip yourself with the knowledge and skills to leverage the power of RL and become a more efficient and innovative coder.

The future of coding is bright with the integration of RL. Embrace the potential of this technology, and embark on a journey of exploration and discovery as you shape the coding landscape of tomorrow!

ABOUT THE AUTHOR

Writer's Bio:

Benjamin Evans, a respected figure in the tech world, is known for his insightful commentary and analysis. With a strong educational background likely in fields such as computer science, engineering, or business, he brings a depth of knowledge to his discussions on emerging technologies and industry trends. Evans' knack for simplifying complex concepts, coupled with his innate curiosity and passion for innovation, has established him as a go-to source for understanding the dynamics of the digital landscape. Through articles, speeches, and social media, he shares his expertise and offers valuable insights into the impact of technology on society.

www.ingramcontent.com/pod-product-compliance
Lightning Source LLC
LaVergne TN
LVHW051539050326
832903LV00033B/4323